Lessons on Demand Presents

Study Guide

Workbook Lessons on

The Boy in the Striped Pajamas

By:

John Pennington

The lessons on demand series is designed to provide ready to use resources for novel study. In this book you will find key vocabulary, student organizer pages, and assessments. This guide is the Student Workbook. The Teachers Guide will have answers and an open layout of the activities. The Student Workbook can be used alone but it will not include answers.

Look for bound print Teacher Editions on Amazon.com

PDF versions can be found on Teacherspayteachers.com

NAME:

TEACHER:

Date:

Vocabulary Box

Definition:

Draw:

Manner

Related words:

Use in a sentence:

Definition:

Draw:

Interrupt

Related words:

Use in a sentence:

Vocabulary Box

Definition:

Draw:

Desolate

Related words:

Use in a sentence:

Definition:

Draw:

Experience

Related words:

Use in a sentence:

Vocabulary Box

Definition:

Draw:

Conviction

Related words:

Use in a sentence:

Definition:

Draw:

Rehearsal

Related words:

Use in a sentence:

Vocabulary Box

Definition:

Draw:

Lacquered

Related words:

Use in a sentence:

Definition:

Draw:

Ergo

Related words:

Use in a sentence:

Vocabulary Box

Definition:

Draw:

Disrespectful

Related words:

Use in a sentence:

Definition:

Draw:

Insolent

Related words:

Use in a sentence:

Vocabulary Box

Definition:

Draw:

Obliged

Related words:

Use in a sentence:

Definition:

Draw:

Criticize

Related words:

Use in a sentence:

NAME:

TEACHER:

Date:

Quiz

Question: Why did the family move?

Answer:

Question: What name did Bruno use when referring to his sister Gretel?

Answer:

Question: What name did Bruno use for the new house?

Answer:

Question: What rank and title was used for Bruno's father?

Answer:

NAME:

TEACHER:

Date:

Assignment: Compare the old and new home.

NAME:

TEACHER:

Date:

Character Sketch

Bruno

Draw a picture

Personality/ Distinguishing marks

Connections to other characters

Important Actions

NAME:

TEACHER:

Date:

Character Sketch

Gretel

Personality/ Distinguishing marks

Draw a picture

Connections to other characters

Important Actions

NAME:

TEACHER:

Date:

Character Sketch

Maria

Personality/ Distinguishing marks

Draw a picture

Connections to other characters

Important Actions

NAME:

TEACHER:

Date:

Research connections

What am I researching? Adolf Hitler

Source (URL, Book, Magazine, Interview)

Facts I found that could be useful or notes

1.

2.

3.

4.

5.

6.

NAME:

TEACHER:

Date:

Draw the Scene: What five things have you included in the scene?

1   2   3

4   5

NAME:

TEACHER:

Date:

Who, What, When, Where, and How

Who

What

Where

When

How

NAME:

TEACHER:

Date:

Vocabulary Box

Definition:

Draw:

Dominate

Related words:

Use in a sentence:

Definition:

Draw:

Tolerant

Related words:

Use in a sentence:

Vocabulary Box

Definition:

Draw:

Evidence

Related words:

Use in a sentence:

Definition:

Draw:

Heritage

Related words:

Use in a sentence:

NAME:

TEACHER:

Date:

Vocabulary Box

Definition:

Draw:

Investigate

Related words:

Use in a sentence:

Definition:

Draw:

Despair

Related words:

Use in a sentence:

NAME:

TEACHER:

Date:

Vocabulary Box

Prospect

Definition:

Draw:

Related words:

Use in a sentence:

Trench

Definition:

Draw:

Related words:

Use in a sentence:

Vocabulary Box

Definition:

Draw:

Diversion

Related words:

Use in a sentence:

Definition:

Draw:

Enthusiasm

Related words:

Use in a sentence:

Vocabulary Box

Definition:

Draw:

Muster

Related words:

Use in a sentence:

Definition:

Draw:

Simpered

Related words:

Use in a sentence:

Create the Test

Question: Why did Bruno need a tyre?

Answer:

Question: What did Bruno and Gretel do with Grandmother, Nathalie every holiday?

Answer:

Question: What did Bruno what to be when he grew up?

Answer:

Question: Who did Bruno meet on the other side of the fence?

Answer:

NAME:

TEACHER:

Date:

Assignment: Compare Bruno and Shmuel

NAME:

TEACHER:

Date:

Character Sketch

Grandmother Nathalie

Personality/ Distinguishing marks

Draw a picture

Connections to other characters

Important Actions

NAME:

TEACHER:

Date:

Character Sketch

Mother

Personality/ Distinguishing marks

Draw a picture

Connections to other characters

Important Actions

NAME:

TEACHER:

Date:

Character Sketch

Father

Draw a picture

Personality/ Distinguishing marks

Connections to other characters

Important Actions

NAME:

TEACHER:

Date:

Character Sketch

Pavel

Personality/ Distinguishing marks

Draw a picture

Connections to other characters

Important Actions

NAME:

TEACHER:

Date:

Research connections

What am I researching? Star of David

Source (URL, Book, Magazine, Interview)

Facts I found that could be useful or notes

1.

2.

3.

4.

5.

6.

NAME:

TEACHER:

Date:

Research connections

What am I researching? Auschwitz

Source (URL, Book, Magazine, Interview)

Facts I found that could be useful or notes

1.

2.

3.

4.

5.

6.

NAME:

TEACHER:

Date:

Precognition Sheet

Who ?

What's going to happen?

What will be the result?

Who ?

What's going to happen?

What will be the result?

Who ?

What's going to happen?

What will be the result?

Who ?

What's going to happen?

What will be the result?

How many did you get correct?

NAME:

TEACHER:

Date:

What would you do?

Character: _____

What did they do?

Example from text:

What would you do?

Why would that be better?

Character: _____

What did they do?

Example from text:

What would you do?

Why would that be better?

Character: _____

What did they do?

Example from text:

What would you do?

Why would that be better?

NAME:

TEACHER:

Date:

Vocabulary Box

Definition:

Draw:

Obvious

Related words:

Use in a sentence:

Definition:

Draw:

Contradict

Related words:

Use in a sentence:

Vocabulary Box

Definition:

Draw:

Catastrophe

Related words:

Use in a sentence:

Definition:

Draw:

Torrent

Related words:

Use in a sentence:

Vocabulary Box

Definition:

Draw:

Sarcasm

Related words:

Use in a sentence:

Definition:

Draw:

Imaginary

Related words:

Use in a sentence:

Vocabulary Box

Definition:

Draw:

Lice

Related words:

Use in a sentence:

Definition:

Draw:

Senile

Related words:

Use in a sentence:

Vocabulary Box

Definition:

Draw:

Sherry

Related words:

Use in a sentence:

Definition:

Draw:

Disguise

Related words:

Use in a sentence:

Vocabulary Box

Definition:

Draw:

Related words:

Use in a sentence:

Unaccustomed

Definition:

Draw:

Related words:

Use in a sentence:

Persuade

Create the Test

Question: What did Pavel do that made Lieutenant Kolter angry?

Answer:

Question: What action made Bruno feel ashamed?

Answer:

Question: Why did Bruno get a haircut?

Answer:

Question: Why did Shmuel bring a set of striped pajamas to Bruno?

Answer:

Assignment: List each chapter title and describe why that title is appropriate.

Character Sketch

Shmuel

Personality/ Distinguishing marks

Draw a picture

Connections to other characters

Important Actions

Character Sketch

Lieutenant Kolter

Personality/ Distinguishing marks

Connections to other characters

Draw a picture

Important Actions

NAME:

TEACHER:

Date:

Character Sketch

Herr liszt

Draw a picture

Personality/ Distinguishing marks

Connections to other characters

Important Actions

NAME:

TEACHER:

Date:

Research connections

What am I researching? Swastika

Source (URL, Book, Magazine, Interview)

Facts I found that could be useful or notes

1.

2.

3.

4.

5.

6.

Top Ten List

1.

2.

3.

4.

5.

6.

7.

8.

9.

10.

NAME:

TEACHER:

Date:

Write a letter

To:

From:

NAME:

Create the Test

Question:

Answer:

Question:

Answer:

Question:

Answer:

Question:

Answer:

NAME:

TEACHER:

Date:

Interview: Who _____

Question:

Answer:

Question:

Answer:

Question:

Answer:

Question:

Answer:

NAME:

TEACHER:

Date:

Advertisement: Draw an advertisement for _____

Chapter to Poem

Assignment: Select 20 words found in the chapter to create a poem where each line is 3 words long.

Title:

_____ _____ _____

_____ _____ _____

_____ _____ _____

_____ _____ _____

_____ _____ _____

NAME:

TEACHER:

Date:

Character Sketch

Name

Draw a picture

Personality/ Distinguishing marks

Connections to other characters

Important Actions

NAME:

TEACHER:

Date:

Comic Strip

Compare and Contrast

Venn Diagram

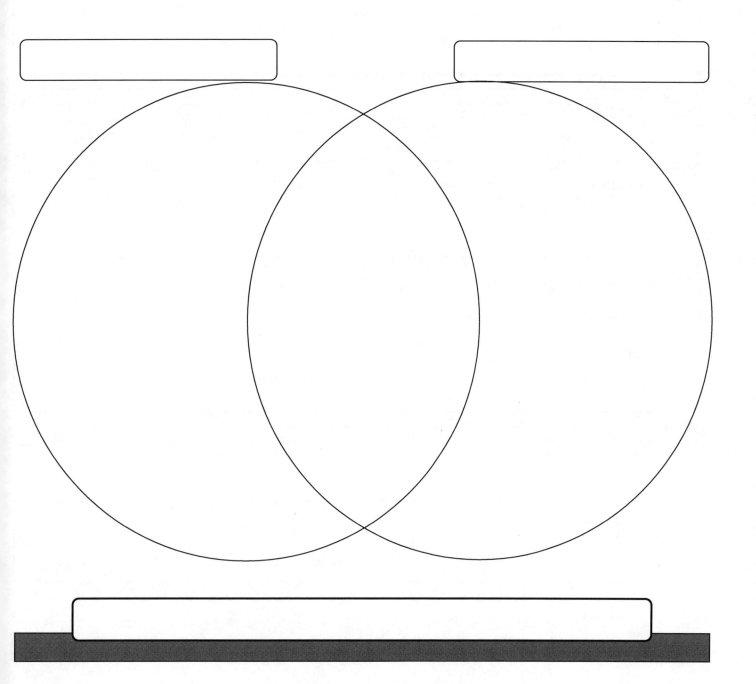

Create the Test

Question:

Answer:

Question:

Answer:

Question:

Answer:

Question:

Answer:

NAME:

TEACHER:

Date:

Draw the Scene: What five things have you included in the scene?

1   2   3

4   5

NAME: _____

TEACHER: _____

Date: _____

Interview: Who _____

Question:

Answer:

Question:

Answer:

Question:

Answer:

Question:

Answer:

Lost Scene: Write a scene that takes place between _____ and
_____

Making Connections

What is the connection?

NAME:

TEACHER:

Date:

Precognition Sheet

Who ?

What's going to happen?

What will be the result?

Who ?

What's going to happen?

What will be the result?

Who ?

What's going to happen?

What will be the result?

Who ?

What's going to happen?

What will be the result?

How many did you get correct?

Assignment: Pyramid

NAME:

TEACHER:

Date:

Research connections

What am I researching?

Source (URL, Book, Magazine, Interview)

Facts I found that could be useful or notes

1.

2.

3.

4.

5.

6.

NAME:

TEACHER:

Date:

1.

2.

3.

4.

5.

Sequencing or timeline

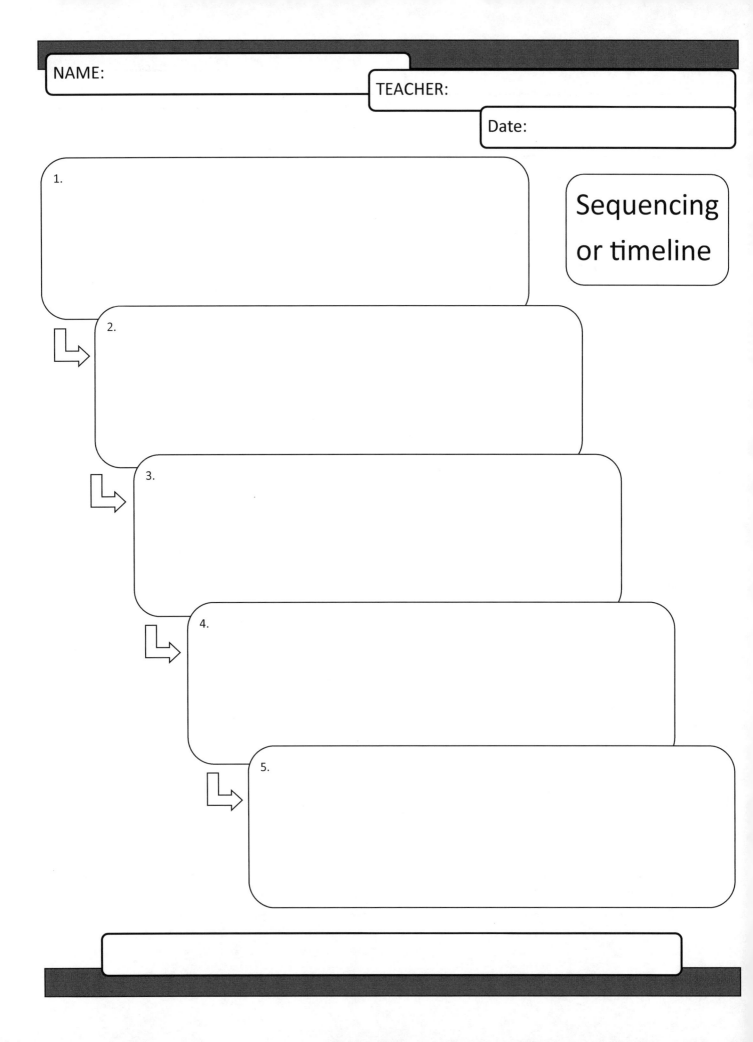

NAME:

TEACHER:

Date:

Support This!

Supporting text

What page?

Supporting text

What page?

Central idea or statement

Supporting text

What page?

Supporting text

What page?

NAME:

TEACHER:

Date:

Travel Brochure

Why should you visit?

What are you going to see?

Map

Special Events

NAME:

TEACHER:

Date:

Top Ten List

1.

2.

3.

4.

5.

6.

7.

8.

9.

10.

Vocabulary Box

Definition:

Draw:

Word:

Related words:

Use in a sentence:

Definition:

Draw:

Word:

Related words:

Use in a sentence:

NAME:

TEACHER:

Date:

What would you do?

Character: _____

What did they do?

Example from text:

What would you do?

Why would that be better?

Character: _____

What did they do?

Example from text:

What would you do?

Why would that be better?

Character: _____

What did they do?

Example from text:

What would you do?

Why would that be better?

NAME:

TEACHER:

Date:

Who, What, When, Where, and How

Who

What

Where

When

How

NAME:

TEACHER:

Date:

Write a letter

To:

From:

NAME:

TEACHER:

Date:

Assignment:

Add a Character

Who is the new character?

What reason does the new character have for being there?

Write a dialog between the new character and characters currently in the scene.

You dialog must be 6 lines or more, and can occur in the beginning, middle or end of the scene.

Costume Design

Draw a costume for one the characters in the scene.

Why do you believe this character should have a costume like this?

NAME:

TEACHER:

Date:

Props Needed

Prop:

What text from the scene supports this?

Prop:

What text from the scene supports this?

Prop:

What text from the scene supports this?

NAME:

TEACHER:

Date:

Soundtrack!

Song:

Why should this song be used?

Song:

Why should this song be used?

Song:

Why should this song be used?

Stage Directions

List who is moving, how they are moving and use text from the dialog to determine when they move.

Who:

How:

When:

Who:

How:

When:

Who:

How:

When:

NAME:

TEACHER:

Poetry Analysis

Date:

Name of Poem:

Subject:

Text Support:

Plot:

Text Support:

Theme:

Text Support:

Setting:

Text Support:

Tone:

Text Support:

Important Words and Phrases:

Why are these words and phrases important:

Made in the USA
Monee, IL
30 June 2024

60973525R00044